IT'S A GAME

WHAT OTHERS ARE SAYING ABOUT
# IT'S A GAME

"This book is an easy read. Simple but deep and thought-provoking as you move through the "game" levels of life. I enjoyed the writing style that seemed like she was speaking personally, directly to me. Ready or not, there are insights on receiving huge answers to simple small questions. How fun to visualize rubbing up against other bubbles. Step into the next level of your life game. NOW."

**Sandra McGill**
Author, Jesus Codes Healing Program

"Gwen Peterson has hit a home run with this book! It offers a "voice" and writing style that will keep the reader smiling and wanting to read more. Serious Spiritual stuff can be both enlightening and fun, as you will discover when you read this book. You won't find another one out there that's like it!"

**Steven Howard**
Author and Spiritual Coach

"Kept my interest. I found it entertaining and a relatable way of conveying some of life's important lessons for happiness and spiritual wellbeing."

**Shelby Peterson**
Seeker

# IT'S
# A GAME

## Winning With Spirit:
## The Ultimate Life Strategy

# Gwen Peterson
## First Edition

© 2024 Gwen Peterson

This publication is designed to provide accurate and authoritative information in regard to the subject matter covered. It is sold with the understanding that neither the author nor the publisher is engaged in rendering legal or other professional services. While the publisher and author have used their best efforts in preparing this book, the purpose of this book is to educate and give suggestions. The authors and publisher shall have neither liability nor responsibility to any person or entity with respect to any loss or damage caused or alleged to have been caused directly or indirectly by the information contained in this book.

Printed in the United States of America

First Edition

ISBN: 979-8-9913379-0-8 – paperback
ISBN: 979-8-9913379-1-5 – eBook

**Interior Design by:**
Chris Treccani
Gwen Peterson

# DEDICATION

Sometimes it is hard to find the words to thank those who have been so near and dear to your heart for so much of one's life. Shelby, Misty, Linda, Becky, Sandra and Helen. Thank you for bringing so much adventure to my life. I love you all.

# CONTENTS

# INTRODUCTION

———

Have you ever read a book or watched a movie with so many moving parts you felt you needed to read or watch it again and again? Each time taking away a new nugget of information or insight? This will be such a book for you. It may not seem like it, but this has a lot of content and will speak to you at different levels and at different times of your life. You will **feel** drawn to read it and reread it.

We have Earth Angels in our lives long before we know what they are. They say or do something that changes us on the inside. One of my professors at Michigan State University was one. I was a freshman frantically trying to pass his class. I needed his help on writing my thesis. He said he would help me although he didn't normally tutor his students. If I was sincere in wanting his help, he would. He started by saying that he would share something with me. Something that I needed to remember in my life.

( Everything in life has three levels. )

Using a book as an example, he explained how the words on the page were the first level. The second level would be the meaning behind the words. The third l evel was the higher meaning behind it all.

His words struck me, but I wasn't sure exactly why he wanted me to know this. The words would come back to me from time to time and I would smile at his wisdom. Now as I sit writing to you, I am again struck by his wisdom.

I have written three books which are laid out in those three levels. This first book, *It's A Game*, is the first level of knowing. Using my professor's analogy, we will work with what you are able to see, touch and feel on this third-dimensional planet. My second book, *Puzzle Pieces*, represents the second level of knowing. It is the *feeling* the words carry, the vibration of Spirit. My third book, *Your Soul Connection*, is the third level of knowing. Your relationship with your Soul. Your relationship with Spirit. Your connection to Divine knowledge and the All-Knowing.

It isn't necessary for you to understand all three levels. Just know that everything in life has three levels of knowing and life can be about learning to navigate them. Together we will explore some ways of looking at our lives from those levels.

# PART ONE:

# IT'S A GAME!

---

A startling event leads to
a lifetime of discovery

# Let's Get Acquainted

---

This book will **not** be an outline of my spiritual journey; that would be somewhat boring. Instead, I hope to give you a different perspective of your life. A perspective on life that I have come to know as Truth. My journey has drastically changed the foundation of what and who I am today. It has occurred in layers. *It's A Game* will be the first layer. I think it makes a little more sense when sharing these topics, to paint it with a little real person correlation and let you hold it up for comparison to your own life experience. How best to gauge life? Not so much from the judgey kind of gauging, but rather a detached kind of thing.

I will try to share with you the highlights of my journey to date and how I came to be sitting here typing away. It will not be a complete telling of my life experience. My journey has been, and continues to be, a crazy path of twists and turns and some of it won't be relevant right now. It is important for you to know that this is **my** journey. Yours, whether you are just discovering it or are much further along, **will** be different.

Your story will be different.

You have probably come to this book because of the many questions you have in your head. Why is life like this? Who am I? Why do I *feel* stuck? As we move through this book, the questions will not stop, but I hope to show how you can find your answers. Let me ask you a question or two. What about your life, are you ready to keep? What beliefs are you going to hold onto for a little while longer? Maybe you aren't ready to answer these just yet. You may find that you need to put this book away for a time to allow yourself to begin processing the words and the *feelings*. Then, when some time goes by, you may *feel* a nudge and wonder, "What became of that book filled with crazy notions?" You will seek it out because you will find that you are ready for more. Or you may resonate with it so thoroughly now, you *feel* pushed to keep reading and embrace your journey from this new perspective. You may feel as if a part of you wants you to know more, with that your journey has started, my friend.

As this book was coming together, it was suggested to lay down a little foundation for the reader. What will this book be about and what can be expected? Heavy questions for a book that has been channeled. For those new to the term channeling and spirituality in general, this book is a lot of both. It is my journey and Spirit's message. I will apologize now if my book makes you shake your head and say, "What?" I did a lot of that myself over the years. It is part and parcel of taking concepts and experiences and finding words to articulate them. I Trust that on a Soul level you will understand because that is why you are reading this book.

Much of this book is channeled from a number of Archangels and Ascended Masters, Spirits from the higher dimensions I have come to know. All wanting to share knowledge with those who are nudged to read this book and play The Game in a more profound way.

Let me share a little more about channeling as I have come to know it. You will find that channelers have a slightly different take on what exactly channeling is, but most would agree that there are two different ways to channel, trance and conscious. Most would agree that channelers and mediums are different in regard to whom they are channeling.

- **Trance channelers** such as Edgar Cayce, Jane Roberts, or more recently, Esther Hicks, completely withdraw their conscious mind and allow Spirit to flow and speak through them. Trance channelers are completely unaware of their surroundings and what is being communicated through them.

- **Conscious channelers** such as yours truly are folks who are, for the most part, aware of their surroundings and share what they are "hearing" from Spirit. They must quiet their mind to listen; many conscious channelers do their listening in a meditative state. The thing to keep in mind with conscious channelers is they are filtering the messages they receive through their belief systems and life experiences. These messages are interpreted by the channeler.

Suffice it to say, I am a conscious channel. That means that I do not withdraw my conscious mind. I do have to quiet my mind as best I can to interpret Spirit's vibrational message. I do not hear their messages with my ears but have learned to interpret their vibrational messages I receive. Some conscious channelers turn the flow of Spirit on and off. I do not. I have trained myself to hold open that channel for information. It is like having an antenna that I didn't have before. If the Archangels and Ascended Masters need to share something, I will hear their vibrational message.

Keeping that antenna tuned to their frequency makes it easy for me to check in on any guidance I may need.

Through my personal practice I have done quite a bit of Soul work that allows me to dialogue with my Soul more fully for guid-ance, as well. Holding the energy of both of these vibrations takes practice and creates an integrated personality of sorts. What you are reading here is not trance channeled material nor my third-dimen-sional mind. It is that blending of Soul and Spirit coming through. Sometimes my mind will jump in and ask questions and judge what I am receiving and *feeling*. Those moments will be shown in thought bubbles to allow you to see how this all flows. Chances are those thoughts will be similar to the ones you are holding.

> Take note while reading: Whenever I use words that are capitalized mid-sentence, it is referencing the Spiritual aspect of the word or the Higher-level meanings, they are not typos. Self, You, Soul, Trust, Love, Friends, for example, are the higher aspects of those words. It allows you to begin playing with the nuances of the multidimensional game you find yourself in.

More about me. I was raised Catholic and went through most of the Sacraments. Don't get me wrong, organized religion has its place. I mention organized religion because what happened to me that day in the car on my way to work wasn't anything we covered in church or catechism. That day would be the turning point for me. It set me on a lifelong endeavor to learn what spirituality is. Many who are committed to an organized religion are quick to point out to those peering into spirituality, how they believe in God and Jesus, heaven and hell. As if a person who begins a spiritual quest leaves all that behind somehow. I have discovered that spirituality is nothing more than a person's personal journey into who and what their beliefs are around God and Jesus, heaven and hell, among a whole host of other concepts that come up like death and rebirth, Love and Trust. Some explore their spirituality while involved in their organized religion and others leave organized religion only to stumble onto their spirituality. I am of the latter. I assure you, having been raised Catholic, channeling Angels and *feeling* nudges from my Soul were not the lessons taught in our weekly catechism class. Instead, it looked and felt more like a good dose of guilt. Guilt about everything. A *feeling* I wanted to be free of. My quest to *feel* better and understand myself led to even more questions that gnawed at me. Where would I find the answers to the unexplained experiences in my life? The church wasn't prepared to offer answers and I soon found I wasn't prepared for the answers that would come from my asking.

Story time. Maybe this will let you see why I was asking questions.

My mom asked me one morning if I wanted to skip school. It seemed a distant relative had passed and mom wanted to know if I would want to go to the funeral with her and my grandma and grandpa. I would have normally jumped at missing a day of high school, but for some reason it didn't *feel* right. Not a guilty *feeling* but an 'uh-oh this *feels* like trouble' *feeling*. I tried to brush it away, but I heard a voice in my head that said, "No." So, I didn't go to the funeral.

Later that day after school, I got strange phone calls from family members wanting to talk to my mom. Strange she wasn't home yet.

"Wasn't she with you at the funeral?? What's up?"

"Nothing, have her call when she gets in."

Finally, my mom calls. She would be home late as she was at the hospital with Grandma and Grandpa. The car they were in was hit in the funeral procession; they were not hurt too seriously but needed to be kept a little while longer for more tests.

It was things like this that made me stop and say, "Hmm, what would have happened if I was in that car?" It was questions like this that made me ponder the bigger questions: why did I *feel* that 'uh-oh' *feeling*, and who said, "No"? It was those very instances I came to know later as channeling. The nudge was from my Soul and the words were from my Angels/Spirit.

Answers weren't easy to come by back then. The few spiritual books that existed were located in the back of the store next to the bathrooms filed under "Wicca." Not front and center and labeled Self-Help. The books at that time seemed to stir up more questions than they answered. There were lots of books on channeling. What is that? People talking to Spirit or crossed-over Loved ones? Only folks in the Bible talk to Angels and God, right? Right?? So confusing.

## Let's Begin

Begin where? Isn't that the question we ask about spirituality? Then some spiritual smartass tells you, "Begin where you are." Like that is helpful in some way. It will be years until its meaning can be fully understood, much less the enormity of its meaning. Spirituality is like that. Big questions with small answers that turnout to be huge answers to small questions.

Yet, that is all that you have. Begin where you are. You will want to take an inventory of what that looks like for you in this moment. It may be a little scary depending on when this question hits you. Addiction, bad romance, there are a lot of things we can get ourselves caught up in. You may very well be reading this book because life isn't exactly what you had hoped for.

Stop for a moment and think about where you are in your life right now and make a few notes. Things to consider: employment, abundance, and relationships. What is happening in your life? It is important to give yourself this moment to reflect.

_____

_____

_____

_____

_____

Then there are the questions. Why did this happen and why should I do anything at all? What is the purpose? Does it really matter? Remember I mentioned the questions will just keep coming. If you like, note them here. You will have your chance to look for these answers later.

I have questions. What about this book? Why am I writing it and for whom? I don't remember signing up to do any of this and I hope speaking engagements aren't the next thing to follow. Do I hear faint whispers that this is not the only book? I think I can hear laughing out there somewhere too. I guess I should start laughing too and you, my friend, will laugh later when you get Spirit's joke in all this.

_____

_____

_____

_____

_____

_____

## Welcome To Gwen's Mind

Hello, Gwen here. Welcome and have a seat somewhere. You are going to take a ride. A chance to get to know who I am so far. You may have already seen that these writings will be full of innuendos, what have yous, and whatnots. Partly or mostly because there is no better way to share with you this journey, which will culminate in a book guided by those you will come to know and written by a person who has found herself caught up in a very strange life experience far from where she thought she would be.

Many of my closest friends and family have no clue of the trials, tribulations, levels of awareness, and not-of-this-world happenings that I have encountered. Until now, I have only shared it with a handful of friends in my spiritual circle. How does someone begin to share such information with those they love and hope not to lose because of our Soul's choices? Better I put it down on paper and let everyone make their choice of whether to see this side of me exposed or not.

There were some really good thoughts on those scraps of paper, so I hope you guys remember what they were! lol

The nudges for this book have been coming for a while now. When I would stop to think about it, I couldn't even start to imagine where it would go or even begin. Pieces have been coming to me and I have written them down on scraps of paper and in journals. Almost all of them have been lost or thrown away over the years. In some distant way I knew that when the time came, I would sit down and tap into my connection with my Non-Physical Friends. The Friends I have come to Know and Trust in such a deep way. Their guidance would flow and make sense to those they are meant for.

Conscious channeling at its best. This has been going on for a number of years, decades, I guess. They have introduced themselves over the years and more come through as the years move on. I am referring to the Archangels, Ascended Masters, and a few others that may get introduced as we go on or not. For the most part, 'They' are who I have come to call the Mentors, Lords of Light, or simply Friends or Spirit. The name is irrelevant; it is just a placeholder for the big explanation of who and what. This group comes through me and steers me

> It has been an interesting ride so far and I have gotten better at being the driver and host.

through so much of my work and day-to-day experiences. They have been so important in the founding of the Spiritual Communities Network, Insights and Illuminations, and my life in general over the past quarter century. Hmmm, I am getting a nudge here reminding me of those moments when I was really young and I was hearing and *feeling* their presence. Funny how we dismiss things and then later look back and go "Oh yeah!" I guess I didn't have the understanding in those younger years and just filed them away.

So far so good, my Friends. I am liking this flow of our story together. Now the conundrum. Where do I want to go from here? My mind wants to take over and decide how this story goes. It wants the words to make sense and follow some rhyme or reason. Perhaps following a specific storyline that has been laid out in a thousand different ways by those who would say how a book should look and sound. But for the moment, I think I will stop. Tomorrow will be another day to pick this up and let Spirit lead. The editing will come later.

Here I sit doing what *feels* like the hundredth time of reading and rereading and I *feel* a nudge. How did we leave out the whole Soul thing? I won't delve too deeply into a conversation about the Soul. Definitely a discussion for another time. Suffice it to say, my

Soul has a very active part in all of this as well. The nudges. Those would be my Soul. Nudge, Nudge, Nudge. Nudge. Nudge.

It is my hope you will see the flow of The Game even as I write this book, listening to Spirit and following the nudges of my Soul as I put this book together. Even though channeling can be a lot of listening, it is also a *game* of paying attention to your life experiences.

For instance, talking with a friend completely independent of my book, they mention a book they heard of called—Are you ready for this? —*The Game of Life and How to Play It* by Florence Scovel Shinn. IKR! You can't make this up. I hear my mind say, "We don't need to continue *this* book as it has already been done." My Non-Physical Friends are quick to point out that it is time for this information to be made relevant again.

I did a little research, you know. The two books will be similar, yet different, in their depiction of The Game. It may sound strange, but it is comforting to know Florence Scovel Shinn's book is out there. If you are reading this book, it all worked out well and I hope you will enjoy the strange way this is strung together. You see, knowledge of Ms. Shinn's book comes after years of beginning to write this book. I am maybe 2/3 of the way through. It is a confirmation for me. A Universal wink if you will that I am on track and need to continue to get this done at this time. I Love Universal winks. They help me sort out my mind and its concerns. The comforting *feeling* is my Soul agreeing with the process. Thank you, Friends, for sending the moral support.

Here is another beautiful slice of serendipity. Ms. Shinn wrote the book at a time when Alice Bailey was busy channeling Djwal Khul a.k.a. The Tibetan a.k.a. DK. Take note as Djwal Khul is part of my spiritual journey too. Just a little FYI and maybe a short story at another time.

Suggestion as we move forward: If you can, don't let your mind try to jump ahead on topics. It may say to you that it knows this stuff already, but I assure you, my Non-Physical Friends involved in the creation of this book are turning a few things on their head and you will want to be cognizant of their subtleties. It may be less confusing that way. Okay, proceed, my friend.

## That Fate Full Day

Often nuggets will come through during my morning meditation practice and I just hop onto the computer, open this file and I skip around and add what is coming through. Today is my writing group day. As I sit looking at the somewhat blank page, I can *feel* the nudge to share the story that is at the root of this book and it causes me a great deal of angst in sharing. Ready, set, go!!

It was sometime during the early 1990s when I was trying to figure out how to get out of the funk, I was in. I seemed so depressed. Why? I had a good paying job—not that I Loved it, but the money was there. I was married. Things seemed good there; we were building our new home and we were excited about that. We were vacationing in beautiful places and I had great friends to hang out with. How is it possible to not be happy? But I wasn't. Not in the deepest part of me. I had for a few years been listening to Jack Boland at Church of Today.[1] He was televised and I had bought a number of his taped talks. An amazing man and teacher. I loved listening to him. He could lift that heavy *feeling*. He made me want to understand what he was saying on a deeper level. I wanted to experience life the way he described it.

Heck, I had a 45-minute drive every day to and from work, so why not listen to my buddy and find my happy spot. This particular morning, as Jack was talking, I hadn't realized I had kind of slipped into a meditative state. (I hadn't begun a meditation practice yet and wouldn't understand this moment for a long time.) From that deep space, I remember just kind of silently shouting at God, "What the hell is this all about anyway? Tell me!! I am tired of *feeling* like this."

Suddenly I was jolted back to reality by a bunch of people yelling, "It's a game!" I quickly realized I had zoned out and was now flying 90mph into a sharp turn on the freeway. I laughed and thought, "Okay, I got my answer and now I am going to die."

## A Game?

I braked heavily, got the car under control, and reflected on what the heck happened. The voices had been so clear and loud like the owners of the voices were sitting in the car with me. As I thought about it more, I noticed that I recognized the voices. Grandma, Grandpa, Harland, Dad, and others. Wait. These people are all dead. Dad died when I was five and I should have no idea what he would sound like. Yet I knew. I knew in my heart of hearts it was him. (As I reread this for editing, I can *feel* his hug and his love fills my heart. Where is my box of tissues?)

What the heck was that!!!

What game? Even though I was asking the question, I was *feeling* the answer. I could *feel* the Truth in the words. I could *feel* some of the heaviness of my funk lifting.

As I continued my drive to work, my body felt really strange. I could *feel* the fabric of my clothes, the actual threads as they crisscrossed to form the fabric. And I could *feel* the pores of the leather that covered my steering wheel. I also began to notice that I was aware of another presence within me staring out of my eyes and taking things in. I could sense a *feeling* that I had never felt

before. Unconditional Love. **The absence of judgment.** It was
the most amazing *feeling* and one
that I knew was not of this world.
It radiated from whatever was
now sharing my body with me. I
observed its observing and I just
sat in that *feeling*, soaking it in
and wishing that I, too, could find
that unconditional loving essence
of that being within myself. Was
that even possible?

When I got to the office, I
called my sister and told her what
was happening to me. Her suggestion was to not tell anyone
about this. I would be locked
up. It would be another ten years

> Now I find myself sitting here writing
> what I have come to know and not quite
> sure what that will look like to you, tell-
> ing a story that until now I have shared
> with very few people. But to share with
> everyone in a book how I continued to
> travel down that rabbit hole and found
> myself thrown deeper and deeper into
> the limitless Love that is Spirit—well,
> that may be a whole different story.
> Some, I am sure, will feel I have blown
> a fuse somewhere. Where will this book
> go now? I think I will step away and let
> this revelation on paper sit.

until I rendezvoused with the people and resources to answer
the bazillion questions I now had. And another ten years to sort
out this Game thing.

## The D&D Metaphor

Funny what you find when you open your eyes to things. I
have pondered in meditation what this book could possibly look
or sound like? All the bits and pieces didn't seem to make sense
to me, and what about 'The Game'? I knew somehow the book
was going to be about The Game we are playing here in the third
dimension and considered the idea that maybe this would incorporate a game. Maybe spelling out the goal of The Game, rules,
directions? I just couldn't see it though. I couldn't *feel* it because I
was too caught up in my mind. I kept thinking about the many

games I have played and which of those would best resemble my mission here. Once I quieted my mind in meditation though, and allowed myself to listen, I felt nudged to check out *Dungeons & Dragons*. I had never played *Dungeons & Dragons* but basically grew up with the knowledge that it was a game that tended to draw in fanatics for it; cosplayers and

> I went to MSU and there were always stories of D&D games being played in the steam tunnels and the urban tales of kids losing themselves in the game and disappearing, never to be heard from again. How would this game be similar to what I am working on?

LARPers (i.e.: live action role-playing where players immerse themselves in their characters and act out their choices, like an unscripted play).

I was *feeling* called to go to the bookstore in search of this game.

I asked my daughter about the game of D&D and she wasn't

> Does the bookstore carry games?

sure it would be helpful as D&D isn't a board game. D&D is made up of books on "how to play the game" as it is a role-playing game, or RPG. LOL Do you see the fun Spirit is having already with this?

So off to the bookstore to see what my next puzzle piece looks like. May I say that it did not let me down. I picked up the *D&D Player's Handbook*. As my daughter said, there were a few books on how to play the game and some game pieces for purchase, but I stuck with the *Player's Handbook*, which appeared to be a very detailed description of the 'game.'

As I flipped the pages, I just laughed. Twenty-five years and here was The Game spelled out in *Dungeons & Dragons*. I guess if I hadn't lived through these years the way I did, the book I was holding wouldn't be resonating with me in the way that it was. It wasn't a book I would be reading in its entirety, yet I could see there was a lot for me to appreciate. I was mesmerized by the synchronicity of things and could *feel* that I had uncovered a big piece of the puzzle and on a much higher level. I purchased the book. My daughter was happy with my decision and eager to get her hands on it when I was done with my research.

> I will let you know now that this book you are holding will NOT have that kind of content.

Let me start by saying how the layout of the *D&D Player's Handbook* is amazing. The work that has been poured into it and the depth of content is, well, amazing, all 300 plus pages.

Like the Shinn book, there are aspects these books will share, but I can *feel* this going in a different direction.

I looked at it from how it was laid out.

> Is this how I should fashion the layout of my book?

I could *feel* it was something more than this. Maybe if I read it, I will see why Spirit directed me to this book. I started with the preface and … wow. The first page I read of the *Player's Handbook* had the most far-reaching depth for me. I could *feel* the words and

> Could I be that inspiring?

Loved the message Mike Mearls shares with the beginners about how to play the game.

I realized I didn't need to read much further. How would I incorporate what I was *feeling* from these words into my book?

## A Cliché

Let me share with you about this past month as I have been haunted by the words of Mike Mearls. So much so that I am using the quote here and hope that I don't break some copyright or plagiarism rules. I truly have to wonder if the folks who created this role-playing game, or RPG, were aware or are aware of the overlap between D&D and the real-life game we play here on planet Earth? I would like to think they do. Okay, here is the part that really haunted me this past month. Mike Mearls writes,

> "The first characters and adventures you create will probably be a collection of clichés. That's true of everyone, from the greatest Dungeon Masters in history on down. Accept this reality and move on to create the second character or adventure, which will be better, and then the third, which will be better still. Repeat that over the course of time, and soon you'll be able to create anything, from a character's background story to an epic world of fantasy adventure. Once you have that skill, it's yours forever."[2]

I hope you can *feel* the depth to these words as it is your Soul's story. The role your Soul plays over and over again in many lifetimes. I suspect I will have reason to revisit this analogy in the future. For now, let's play with cliché.

The word just kept going around and around in my head. It touched my Soul. Mr. Mearls' use of the word cliché. It kept popping up in the work I do. Often, I *feel* called to step out of my comfort zone and do something I know nothing about. One such thing is writing social media posts. I want to create engaging posts on social media. I really want to be inspiring with my words. At first, the words are those that have been used a million times and are, OK, boring, or cliché. But as I keep working at it, the words are starting to flow easier, and with time they will have more depth and meaning. When I hear the word cliché echo back at me when I begin a new project, I *feel* relieved that I don't have to be a master out of the gate.

Fast forward. I am still writing this book (lol) and am sitting in my writing group today. I didn't *feel* any great information to write and opted for a little editing. Read, reread, look for some type of flow so as not to lose you. Having read the above paragraphs, written a couple of years ago, I am struck by these words again. Do I mention my sixtieth birthday is tomorrow? When I was young, sixty seemed so old. Today COVID-19 continues on, my divorce is final, my mother has transitioned, and I have cut cords with toxic relationships, to name a few of the many things that have happened so far this year. I have had a lot of new beginnings and every time I began to doubt myself or kick myself for not being perfect, the word cliché would pop in and I would take a deep breath and allow myself to move through it without the need to be perfect. In this moment, I am the freest I have ever been on so many levels of my being. I *feel* very young and *feel* I am reinventing myself. Who do I want to be when I grow up? I am excited to be creating a new life story. Such a far cry from the girl in the car.

Spirit is sharing with me that this book will be a lot like the cliché. It will be very general on a number of topics. Somewhat third dimensional in its telling. It is meant to give you the lay of the land and confidence to begin playing The Game. I suspect this gentle reminder is also a heads-up to me that there will be other books to come that will address the higher levels of work I do. It will be interesting to see how this work will tie in with the classes I have been teaching. I can *feel* a gentle unfolding of something much bigger than I am able to fully grasp in this moment. Can you *feel* it too?

# A Reminder

A quick reminder as you get ready to read and digest the information presented in Part Two. My interpretation of The Game has come through years of my own spiritual practice and I continue to discover new Truths. What I share is what I have learned and continue to practice in my day-to-day living. Am I perfect at The Game? No, there are times I *feel* like a cliché. Other times I see miraculous things happen in my life and I question how these things are possible. There are things I have been taught to believe are impossible. I want to believe they are possible. I have found questions like: who am I, what is this all about, why is this happening, are nudges of the Soul for me to go deeper into learning who I am.

My meditation and journaling practice set the stage for so much of my understanding about spirituality. Spirit has nudged me toward materials to read that were confirmations for what I was learning from Spirit. My personal experiences taught me to Trust my Soul and Spirit. Learning to allow myself to *feel* the loving presence of my Soul has been an incredible journey that continues to make itself manifest in my life.

Spirituality is not a one-and-done thing. It is ever growing and evolving. As you read Part Two, take time to see how you *feel*. What things resonate with you and which ones don't. Find a quiet place to sit with your reactions. Some of what I share may rub against old belief systems. Is it time to let those go? Only you can know that answer. It is my hope to empower you in finding **your** answers. Don't let anyone tell you. you can't. If something I say resonates in your heart, play with it. If it doesn't, move on. The beauty of The Game is you and your Soul learning to play together.

PART TWO

# Let's Begin to Setup The Game

─────

As with any game, you eagerly open it up. You pull out the instructions and read them to better understand how the game will be played: how many players can play, how to set up the game board, and so on. Sometimes you find the instructions on the inside of the lid. The games I have purchased recently have instruction booklets. Consider this your instruction booklet to playing this Game we call life.

Ready?

## Game Pieces

Each of these are capable of becoming very lengthy discussions in and of themselves. We will discuss these in greater detail later. For now, let's get the lay of the land with a simple explanation of each. Some of these you have heard me use and may have an understanding of already.

**Avatar** - You and Other Physical Players

**Soul** - The Eternal You.

**The Mind** - The thing you think with all day.

**Ascended Masters** - Souls that have mastered The Game.

**Angels** - Non-Physical higher-dimensional beings.

**Guides** - Many of the indigenous peoples relate to Spirit Guides versus Ascended Masters and Angels. I often call all of these higher beings guides.

**Third Dimension** - The tangible universe we live in.

**God** - All-That-Is, White Light, Unconditional Peace, Love, and Joy. There are many names, we will use God in this book.

# Setting Up the Board

This part you really don't need to worry about. There are many game boards being played on many dimensions but for this particular Game we will focus on third-dimensional planet Earth. It has already been set up for you to begin playing the day you were born.

What is the big deal about the third dimension? A lot of people talk about it and reference it. Some may have a vague knowledge of what it really is. It helps to have a strong understanding of what the third dimension is and is not.

In the third dimension:
- Vibrational energy moves really slow.
- We have the ability to touch and taste.
- 'Things' exist.

- Time and space exist.
- We use a thing called the mind to follow cause and effect.
- 'Things' appear to be solid.
- The appearance of death happens.
- We create limitations like age, time, money, and education.
- Thoughts/beliefs become things.
- We believe in darkness.

All the above give us a linear game board to play in. The above items only exist in the third dimension. The higher dimensions have faster moving energy, causing things to lose their solidness and time, space, bodies, minds and such, for the most part, do not exist. That is what makes this the perfect place for Spirit and our Souls to play. It is so completely different from any other dimension. Maybe think of it in terms of the straw that breaks the camel's back. The camel goes along and then it is the one straw that changes everything. Monkeys go along like monkeys do and then the one-hundredth one changes everything. That is the third dimension. The straw. The one-hundredth monkey. The place of time and space. Instead of everything happening all at once in a primordial soup of energy constantly morphing in all ways at all times, Vibrational energy pretty much comes to what would appear to be a grinding halt or suspended animation. Welcome to your game board.

> Is this where I need to interject one of my many personal experiences that ground some of these ideas into my mind in such a way that I couldn't argue with it unless I wanted to call myself crazy? I can feel the nudge to continue. It is funny because I hadn't thought of that moment in a really long time.

A really long time ago, I was having one of my deeper meditations where I was communing with Spirit. Letting my mind observe the higher dimensions with my Soul. This was an experience unlike any I had had before. It is when I met Mother Mary. I know, I know it sounds crazy. I can *feel* my ego alarm going off as I type this memory for you. In fact, that was what brought me out of my meditation. My mind had become active and was like, "What was that?" When I opened my eyes and began to anchor back into my body, I felt really different, almost like the car ride that changed my life. As I got up to move around, I felt like I was moving through water. I am not a diver, but I have sat on the bottom of a pool. That is the *feeling* I was having. The air was so tangible and heavy that I thought I could float if I wanted to. In that moment, I realized what 3D really was. Very slow, dense moving energy. To this day, I ask myself, could I have floated if my mind would have let me?

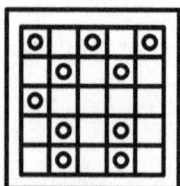

Keep the idea that 3D is just slow-moving energy in mind going forward with this book.

# Players of The Game

## The Avatar

You, my friend, are the avatar. It is the physical beingness that you call you. The body that you can touch and feel and see in the mirror.

Let's stop for a moment and visit with your avatar. Of course, this isn't an exhaustive list but it will get you started in thinking about you, the avatar. Here are a few suggestions.

Begin with your physical appearance:
- The easiest and most obvious is the race you chose.
- What about your nationality?
- Your sex and your relationship with it.
- Move on to hair. Consider the color and type or lack thereof.
- Eye color.
- Body size and shape.

Doing good so far. Time to go a little deeper with:
- Religious upbringing and affiliation.
- Family or lack of family is another determining factor for your Game piece.

Let's go deeper still and add into the mix your life experience to date:
- Education level.
- Income level.
- Marital status.
- Health.

Stop now and begin to describe your avatar. This may be good fodder for a journaling session as you can go pretty deep into this, if you choose. Find more paper if you need it.

_____

_____

_____

_____

_____

_____

_____

## The Soul

Heads up on this one. If you are coming to this book not knowing much about spirituality at this point, give me a moment to paint a little background of what I have come to know about the Soul. It may get deep pretty quick, so pace yourself and let yourself process how you *feel* about what I am sharing. It is not necessary for you to embrace all of this in one sitting. See what *feels* good to you and put the stuff that doesn't on the back burner. Maybe make a note to yourself to revisit it.

Consider the fact that you are sitting here with this book in hand because of your Soul. Your Soul is the eternal part of you, the part that never seems to age. It is as much a part of you as the avatar you described earlier. Your relationship with your Soul comes through as emotions. As we become aware of our Soul, we are able to build a dialogue of sorts with it. The Game allows us to observe ourselves, our mind, and our thoughts and live life more from the Soul's perspective. A perspective that allows us to see the various games going on and understand more fully that The Game of Life is not happening to us, but rather we are actively playing The Game and influencing it.

Okay, we have a Soul but what **is** the Soul? The Soul **is** Vibrational energy **and** an extension of God. Stepped down energy because we are in the 3D world of slow-moving energy, but it is still made up of Unconditional Love, Peace, and Joy energy that is God. We tend to *feel* our Soul in our heart center. For instance, whenever you experience something that makes your heart sing, *feel* full of Love, or moves you to tears, that is you resonating with your Soul. You are in what is called alignment with your Soul. Other times it can come through as a hollow *feeling*. Like there is something missing. Maybe a sense that something needs to be done. This is your Soul attempting to get your attention because you are focusing on something not in alignment with who you are and brings less than Peace, Love, and Joy. This awareness is the beginning of building a relationship with your Soul.

A little bit more about the Soul before we move on. Your Soul resides in dimensions that are not linear. It is in an eternal now moment. A now moment for your mind would be like not thinking about the past or future. Instead, being present in what is happening right here, right now, taking in all the senses at once without any of the limitations of the 3D. Don't worry if your mind isn't ready to go there just yet. That is where the Soul comes into play because from its vantage point, it is in the eternal now moment and has access to Divine Wisdom. It already knows your past, future, and highest good and chose this very life experience.

## God

Let me give a little background on the role God plays in The Game, or rather what God isn't. In The Game, God is not vengeful or a man sitting on a throne somewhere casting judgment on all. He is not tallying points for condemnation on judgment day.

Instead, begin to play with the idea of an infinite unconditional loving presence; Vibrational energy really. But if it helps to think of it as a "him" or other anthropomorphic being, that is fine as long as it is infinite Unconditional Love, Peace, and Joy. God is in and through all things. There isn't anything that you can point to that isn't God's energy in some form. Maybe you are *feeling* a fuzzy *feeling* in your heart center?? That is, you resonating with your Soul's Truth and feeling God's Love.

What is the relationship between your Soul and God? I asked this same question of Spirit one day and it was explained to me like this. Consider your body as a representation of God. Now as your attention travels to the fingertips, you are traveling through the slower moving dimensions of Spirit. Ultimately, the very tip of your finger is your Soul in the third dimension. As the finger and fingertips have their experiences, so does God. It is through the Soul that God is able to experience itself. Over seven billion ways and that is just here on this planet. Did I give you too much at once? Revisit with this later. Let's move on.

## The Mind

Ah, the mind. The thing you think with all day long and won't let you sleep at night. It is exclusively found here in The Game and attempts to keep control of the avatar. It is what anchors your Soul to this game board.

What makes each avatar unique and brings lots of depth to The Game is the mind. It has been studied and dissected. It has been tested and electrocuted. It has been given lots of names and attributes, like ego, consciousness, subconscious, and so on. Many books have been written and therefore, I will not go into those details here.

Let's keep it light and simple for the essence of The Game. Without the mind, your avatar can't get things done. It is the part of us that identifies with "who we are." The mind creates habits, thoughts, rationalizes, holds beliefs, and interacts (all those things you sometimes wish it wouldn't). It is quite able to operate on its own and is a very useful tool in 3D.

There are a few things you want to keep in mind though about your mind. *Pardon the pun. lol*

- **It should NOT be allowed to run on autopilot**, or say, unattended. We don't really begin to understand this rule until we become self-aware. That awareness thing I talked about earlier. The moment when your Soul begins to get your mind's attention and causes it to say something like, "Hey, what or who was that?"

  As you grow and get to know these two halves of the 3D whole that is you, you begin to see how much the mind is a lot like a three-year-old child. Meditation and journaling practices really accentuate this and is the reason why so many people give up. Who really wants to willingly sit for any length of time with a whining three-year-old? Just look at the parents of a three-year-old. It takes a lot of moxie to hold the course. Getting your mind under control is one of the biggest aspects of The Game because you really don't want an unattended three-year-old running your life.

- **It only knows the past.** Your mind has been fed a diet of fear over the years and has become very fearful as a result. It is ready to regurgitate past failures, losses, and injuries. The mind also knows that its days are numbered. This just adds to the fear component of The Game.

- **It cannot see into the future** and therefore—you guessed it—it can be very afraid of the future.

- **Any changes in your life experience can scare your mind** and begin a thread of fearful thoughts that end with, "and then we will die." Without even thinking about it, we usually cut the mind off when it begins this downward spiral. But "stuffing" these fearful thoughts away doesn't stop them, either consciously or unconsciously. Think minimizing your open pages on your phone or computer. They're still running.

Ah, the unconscious mind rears its head. Round and round your mind will go, waiting for the most inappropriate moment to explode like a stink bomb or hand grenade. You know, like a three-year-old having a temper tantrum. You've seen it. Someone didn't get a napkin in their to-go order and the explosion begins. Anyone standing near takes a step back. All those stuffed down emotions exploding everywhere.

- **The mind is happiest** when it has a job to do and is reassured that all is well.
- **GIGO-Garbage in, garbage out**. Whatever the mind has been fed, it will regurgitate. Fear, hate, Love, Peace, or Joy.

# Non–Physical Players

This section can be a little tricky. It can push a lot of belief buttons your mind holds depending on the life experience to date. Some minds may have yielded enough to allow the entertaining of Non-Physical beings to exist. Some were raised with this knowledge. Still others find themselves thrown into it, ready or not.

Below I will talk about some Non-Physical players you may meet as you play The Game. I usually refer to them collectively as Spirit, Guides, Friends, or Mentors. The name is not important as it is a placeholder for those higher-energy beings that are not in physical form. This is not a complete list of Non-Physical beings we interact with on a higher level, but I think you will have your hands full with these players for now.

Earlier I spoke about how various topics, this book, and your life can cause deep questions to come up. This topic around the Non-Physical players caused me to question the who, what, and why of these players in our life experience. This is how my Non-Physical Friends explained it:

Before this life experience, your Soul was hanging out with its Non-Physical Friends (Angels, Guides, Ascended Masters, and such). As everyone was hanging out, it was suggested to take a road trip. Your Soul agreed to be the driver of the vehicle (you, the avatar) and your Non-Physical Friends would be there with you, ready to give direction. They agreed to only step in when called upon by the Soul. No one likes a back seat driver, right? The road trip being this Game right now with you.

Imagine if you will, trying to drive a car that has a mind of its own and your Friends are in the back seat having a good old time waiting for you to ask for help. Yeah, that's The Game. And here you sit right in the middle of it.

You may have encountered one of these amazing Non-Physical beings coming through a physical player. I know you have met them. Those amazing folks who say just the right thing at the right moment and it pierces your heart in a good way. The essence of their words or actions stays with you and years later you realize that they were a guidepost, a sign to direct you to your Soul. They caused you to shift and it meant everything to your life experience. Yep, they were your Angels and Guides reaching out to you.

Let me introduce you to some of your travel companions.

## Angels

This conversation can get deep really quick. For now, let's keep it simple. There are Angels. Lots and lots of Angels doing all kinds of things on many dimensions. Their Vibrational energy is only slightly stepped down from that God energy we are all a part of. Remember, Infinite Unconditional Love, Peace, and Joy Energy?

Some names you may recognize are Michael, Metatron, and Rafael. Let me tease you with the idea that these are the male aspects and Angels are both male and female, just like your Soul. Some of the ranking of Angels include Archangels and Seraphim. All are available to assist your Soul.

Angels cross many dimensions. They transcend the trappings of the mind because, well, they don't have an avatar to cruise around in. They are Divine Wisdom.

They have dedicated themselves to serving/supporting each and every Soul on its adventure. Some folks are able to see them, and some train themselves to do so. Or they, like me, have come to hear them, both clairaudient and vibrationally. We all have them. They are ever present. Remember my analogy about taking the road trip. These are your party buddies who came along for the ride and are waiting for you to invite them in to help along the way. Their role is to steer your mind to your Soul. They help you to learn how to Trust that which you are and *feel* the Unconditional Love that is there for you and is part of you. Sometimes they will jump in and move something that needs to be moved but usually they are there to point the way and have a good laugh with you. Sometimes it will *feel* like it's a good laugh at you.

> They do that too, I'm sure, but it is with the limitless Love of God.

I recently had a conversation with someone who was sharing how Spirit put something in their way to punish them. NO! That is not how The Game works. We are talking Unconditional Love, Peace, and Joy. Spirit/God/Soul does not punish us or 'teach' us lessons. What we do have is free will and that just adds to the fun or complexity of The Game. Okay, just needed to be clear on this.

This probably belongs in the Rules section too.

## Guides and Ascended Masters

Probably the easiest way to differentiate Angels from the Spirit Guides and Ascended Masters is that Angels have a higher frequency or energy about them as a result of their proximity to God energy and are able to transcend the highest dimensions.

Spirit Guides and Ascended Masters have lived many lifetimes and have mastered The Game. They have transcended the mind and are able to create what we would call miracles because they are without the limitations of the mind. Insert "Dungeon Master" and discussion on clichés reference.

A number of Ascended Masters have come through to me over time and have helped me come to know my Soul in ways I never knew possible. To experience the essence of Love, Peace, and Joy and realizing that we have no way of conceiving of the infiniteness of God's Unconditional Love, Peace, and Joy.

In writing this, I could feel the flutter of my heart center. Did you feel it, too, as you read those words?

Let me introduce my Friends and coauthors: Jesus, St. Germain, Merlin, Quan Yin, Lady Nada, Mother Mary, White Buffalo Calf Woman, White Tara, Melchizedek, Djwal Khul, and Kuthumi. This by no means is a complete list of AMs or Guides. Rather, these are the ones that have come forth through my work to guide me and have had a heavy hand in the creation of this book. They come together in a blended energy with the Archangels. My mind is wanting to jump in and explain more about these Masters, but for now I feel we will move on.

## Other Avatars

All those people you see moving around you, family, friends, and those you have not actually met on the 3D board yet. All avatars playing their own game. Like you, they move around in their little bubbles of their own making. Sometimes we play a game or two with them and some we won't.

**Helpful tips when encountering another avatar:**

- You cannot create in another's game bubble. You may influence them by rubbing up against their bubble, but no one creates in another's bubble.
- No two avatars are having the same life experience.
- Life experiences color the way we see our life, kind of like filters on a camera.
- As a result of these filters/perspectives, no two avatars are seeing The Game board in the same way. Imagine over seven billion perspectives of the same game board. It is a miracle we navigate this game at all.
- It is important to know that you are not capable of knowing what is in another avatar's mind or see life from their perspective. Sometimes we *feel* like we can or should, but you can't.

- Some avatars have old Souls that have played many a Game and others have newer ones.
- Multiple Souls, Soul Families, and Twin Flames? Great topics for a deeper dive.

## Rules of The Game

Avatar you have been taught to play by certain rules/laws while others were omitted. Let's discuss some of these.

- Rules that tend to involve limitations of time, abundance, age, education, and such are third dimensional. They began as a thought, then entrenched themselves as beliefs and social mores. These rules and laws are always changing and different based on where you choose to live in the world. They do not exist in other dimensions.
- You may not be aware of Universal Laws, which are completely different. These Laws are based on Vibrational energy. They don't change, are always in effect, and exist on all dimensions. Two very important ones to know are:
  o The Law of Attraction- Like attracts like. Your Vibrational energy attracts the vibrational match to that energy.
  o The Law of Focused Thought- You are creating whatever you put your focus on.

These Universal Laws are the basis for everything in the physical and Non-Physical. Put your attention on the thing you want and get in a really good-*feeling* place about it. Sounds easy enough, right? Learning how to finesse these Laws will make playing The Game a real (pardon the pun) game changer. In Part Three, I will talk more on how to integrate this knowledge into your game.

- You can't get it wrong. As much as we have been conditioned to believe that, we can't. It always works to our advantage, if we choose to see it.

# Object of The Game

All game instructions include the Object of The Game. What is the goal? What is to be accomplished? How do you know if you have won The Game? When does The Game end? Questions that all revolve around the idea of what makes playing The Game all worthwhile.

I hope that in describing the Object of The Game, I answer those questions and color it in with a little shift of perspective. Perhaps nudging you to rethink how you come at your life or The Game. Are you done with having your life come at you? Do you want to take on The Game and really play it? Let's find out.

> I suspect that there have been a few avid game players who have stuck with me to this point and may be wondering what the object of The Game is.

## What is the object of The Game?

First off, the goal is to have fun! It is a game after all. Lighten up!

I drive my family crazy by saying that on game night. I am usually met with answers like, "Only losers say that" or "I guess you don't want to win." Neither is true as they usually find out. Those are statements that shed a little light onto how someone comes at their life or how they are playing The Game. Can you *feel* the heaviness in those statements? Sure, they were trying to be funny, but isn't the adage; in every joke is a bit of truth? I play for the experience of having fun, win or lose and so does your Soul.

Often, I hear people say that the reason we are here is to learn lessons or our Souls can't move on. How about, our Souls need to clear their Karma or be healed? Does that sound like fun? Keep in mind, our Souls are here for the experiences and they play from a place of Infinite Joy, nothing more. Souls are not being punished and are most definitely not here to correct their wrongs. They chose to play The Game. Remember you can't get it wrong and neither does your Soul. More advanced Soul's just play more complicated games.

Maybe a more fun way to approach this game is to imagine these so-called "lessons" as puzzle pieces received by the avatar. Each piece gives a clearer picture to the level of Game being played by your Soul(s). If you Love to play video games, then think about video game levels here. You unlock new tools and super powers as you move to new levels gathering up coins.

## What are you trying to accomplish?

Avatar, do you *feel* like you need to be accomplishing something? Then your Soul has a mission. Your Game can be all about figuring out what it is your Soul is trying to accomplish in this short life span it chose. Some may seem insignificant (which they aren't) and others grandiose and what legacies are built on. Don't judge yourself or your Soul. Remember, your Soul is coming from Infinite Joy and you can't get it wrong. Relax and allow yourself to have this experience. In Part Three, I will help you to begin this discovery.

## Who wins?

Is winning The Game still a thing for you at this point? I hear your mind saying, "How do you know if you won The Game?" There is no win or lose here. I hear you. I hear you grumbling and

groaning because some folks have that competitive edge.
How's this? You will know how you are doing by how you are
*feeling*. AAAAAGHHHH! I know someone just blew a gasket
somewhere with that one. Take a deep breath and hear me out.


If you *feel* good most of the time, you are winning. How
you *feel* is an indicator of how well your Soul is shining through
your avatar. If you and your Soul have become best buds, you
will be *feeling* lots of Love, Peace, and Joy in your days. You will
*feel* like a winner.

## When does The Game end?

For the avatar, when you draw your last breath. For your Soul?
It doesn't. It is Infinite. Your Soul will choose another avatar somewhere here on Earth or who knows where. It may happen right
away or not ever. There are many, many, many levels to The Game.
We only scratched the surface with what I have covered so far. I
know that on a certain level of your being you can *feel* how deep
this Game can go.

# PART THREE

# Let's Play

———

Have you enjoyed Spirit's whimsical way of getting you to think about a new perspective on living here on third-dimensional planet Earth? Were you surprised by some of it? This perspective came to me over time through my spiritual practice. It was a process that took time. Small steps that sometimes seemed too small to matter and went no place, and then suddenly opened up to a new level of understanding that changed my life over and over. Let me reiterate, though. It took time. It took commitment at times. It took learning to Love and Trust myself. It wasn't always easy or pretty.

It has been worth every step. Looking back, I don't think I would have gotten to where I am now if I had known where this would be heading. It would have been too overwhelming. I know I am not done learning how to play The Game. I am happy that my Soul knows the way. I don't need to know everything. Just where the next step is. This book is one of those steps. One of many with more still to come and I Love that I get to share it with you.

Here we are. Our avatars sitting on the Start Space. Earlier in Part Two, you were asked to describe your Game Piece. Who are you, avatar? Stop in this moment and go back to that section on the avatar and look at who you are. Who is this avatar your Soul chose? After you *feel* satisfied with your description, come back.

Now, let's look at your Game Piece. Are you male, female, gender neutral, or other? What's your race? Were you born with special needs? These answers begin to show you the avatar your Soul chose coming into this game, like it or not. These attributes will influence The Games both of you enter into. These will be the filters your avatar will see things through. Sure, you can change some of these filters, but that comes later in The Game when you delve deeper into the beliefs you have, your ability to recognize these filters and consciously decide to change them. Reflect back on "A Cliché." Start general, and then with time, add deeper dimensions to your knowledge of The Game, who your avatar is and what your Soul is wanting to experience.

For now, humor me in the idea that your Soul did, in fact, know what this life would be about and actively chose to participate in This Game, at this time, and in this body knowing, full well what it would encounter, and that you would be sitting here right now, not sure what all this means. Wait. Did you *feel* that? There it was again. That *feeling* in your heart center and maybe a tickle in your body somewhere. Maybe thrill bumps? Maybe a fuzziness in your brain? Your Soul and Spirit are making themselves known to you, Avatar. How fun is that?

Are you ready to begin playing The Game in a more intentional way? Are you wondering what to do with all the information laid out about The Game? Wondering where do you even start with all of this? Maybe your mind has snuck in to say, "You don't have time for this. You have too much going on. Life is just too crazy to play games." If so, maybe revisit with the intro to the mind, because it will be always present and ready to jump in to convince you to stop. How do I know? Because that is how the mind works and that is how The Game is played.

Now that we addressed that little interruption … Are you ready to begin?

Silence? Then you are ready to begin.

## Where to Start?

It is hard to say when someone will begin their spiritual journey. It is a very personal and unique experience. It begins as an awareness. An awareness of You. Noticing there is more than one voice running around in your head. One *feels* good and the other does not. The journey has begun.

I want to make something clear as we delve into this. Being born into your life experience with 'gifts' is not the same as a spiritual journey or spirituality. I have met many people who have shared how they have had special abilities since a young age and yet their spirituality was fairly non-existent. Remember that spirituality is nothing more than a person's personal journey into who they are and what they believe. As a person unravels their spirituality, they may uncover some abilities, but those abilities are not spirituality. They are layers of The Game being played. Two very different topics. Spirituality is the practice of self-discovery. A spiritual journey is coming to know Divine Wisdom and Trusting in All-That-Is with all your being. It isn't a box you tick off your list. It becomes how you see your life and live your life. Your personal lifestyle that you intentionally create with your Soul.

As we begin our spiritual journey, we begin to play The Game from a slightly higher vibrational place. A higher Knowing. Not so physical, linear, and tangible. We go through a seeking period. We can't seem to read enough or attend enough classes. We find ourselves *feeling* our lives from a new place and sometimes that can *feel* pretty darn amazing compared to where we were emotionally when we started. Or it can *feel* like a lot of work depending on your life experience to date.

We are beginning to learn about life's higher meaning, that second level my professor spoke of. Sometimes seekers mistake learning about spirituality as being spiritual. Again, two different things. Spirituality is the practice of self-discovery. It bears repeating. Think of it like getting a bike and reading about what a bike is and how to ride it. You can't claim to **know** how to ride a bike until you put your butt in the seat and start to pedal. You can read about spirituality but until you begin your own personal practice, you don't **Know** spirituality.

And yet it will be your own personal spiritual practice, unlike anyone else's. As you begin to be more intentional about you and your relationship with your Soul, you will really start to play The Game instead of The Game playing you. Many students have described their lives as coming at them and not having any control over it. Your spiritual practice will show you the illusion. You were always the creator.

What does a spiritual practice look like? Get ready. A lot of people cringe when I say these words. Meditation and journaling. Yep. These are the foundations to a sound spiritual practice and a great way to see and learn The Game. Think of them as the doorway to The Game. It is how to become acquainted with your Soul and the other Non-Physical players playing with you. These practices are found at the heart of all organized religions. Did I just hear your mind start to chime in again? Assure your mind that you are just going to do some reading and you're not committing to anything right now. No need to get all in a bunch, yet.

## The Art of Meditation

We have all seen it. The word meditation conjures up the image of a yogi sitting in the lotus position for days. Monks in caves for lifetimes. Worse yet, if you tried it yourself, you probably gave yourself a FAIL. I can hear the whining now, "Why is this so important anyway?" I hear you. I know firsthand the internal strife that comes with the mere mention of a meditation practice. I remember when I started and I have heard it from my students for decades. It's too hard. Too hard to sit quietly, too hard to find the time, too hard. I know. I know. I, too, struggled with learning how to meditate, what it was, why it was important. And why was it so hard?

With time, I discovered what meditation really is and what it can and can't do. I have been teaching thousands of folks how to successfully have their own meditation practice. A meditation practice is the spiritual journey. It is getting on the bike and going for a ride.

Let me throw this at you. Without a meditation practice, when will you have the time to sit and hear all that is in your head? Go ahead, guess. When you go to bed. That's right. Can't fall asleep because you can't quiet your mind? Time to think about meditating.

Meditation has been linked to a lot of health benefits. Thorpe and Dasgupta discuss 12 science-based benefits of Meditation as[3]

1. Reduces Stress
2. Controls Anxiety
3. Promotes Emotional Health
4. Enhances Self-Awareness
5. Lengthens Attention Span
6. May reduce age-related memory loss
7. Can generate kindness

8. May help fight addictions
9. Improves sleep
10. Helps control pain
11. Can decrease blood pressure
12. Accessible anywhere

Here's some food for your mind. According to Pew Research, 40 percent of Americans meditate at least once a week.[4] Additionally, Keely shares that of those who meditate, 70% have been doing it for less than two years.[5]

Maybe if I share what it looked like for me at the beginning, you will *feel* a little bit more relaxed. Roughly five years after 'the incident on the way to work,' nothing had really changed by way of a spiritual practice. I felt I was doing everything the way everybody said you had to do it. You go to school, you graduate, go to college, graduate, get a job, buy a big house, dog check, kid check, husband check. Not necessarily in that order. All of this was supposed to make you happy, right? But I wasn't. I was kind of curious as to why that was, because I was playing by the rules and I was not *feeling* that Joy inside that I was craving. I felt this void, a kind of emptiness, a hollow *feeling* in the middle. Like something was missing and I couldn't put my finger on it.

I had heard a lot about meditation. I heard a meditation practice helps with all that stuff. I wasn't quite sure how and it was a difficult decision. I was a corporate America, multitasker, Type A personality. The idea of sitting for ten minutes made no sense. I could get so much done in ten minutes. Sitting, doing nothing went against every fiber of my being. But again, I just really wanted to change whatever was going on in my life and find a happy place to be with it.

I decided to give it a try. I decided to start with guided meditations. I felt they would be a good way to distract my mind seeing it was not on board with any of this. I knew once my day got going, stopping would be really hard so I decided I would sit first thing in the morning on Monday, Wednesday, and Friday. I found that I would fall asleep during the recorded meditations and decided to begin listening to the guided meditations to go to sleep at night too.

After a short time, I realized I was enjoying the down time. The guided meditations were making me *feel* more relaxed as I went into the day and my sleep was improving. I was *feeling* better overall. I decided I was going to increase it to Monday through Friday and give myself the weekend off because my mind was still not quite sold on the whole thing. That's right, I was making compromises with myself. I would do Monday through Friday and for doing such a good job my mind gets the weekend off. It didn't take very long before I started realizing that by Monday when I'd sit down to meditate, my days were a little crazy; that over the weekend all heck was breaking loose. It wasn't going as smoothly as my weekdays were. I was actually happier and calmer during the week than I was on my weekends. I suddenly realized during one of my meditations that it was the meditation helping to calm things down. I couldn't ignore it. My mind did not want to give up the weekend. It still wanted to be in control. Light bulb moment. Meditation is the practice of reigning in the mind. Me and my mind had a little talk. I told my mind, "You know what? When you're on your own, things don't go so smoothly. We are going to continue with our meditation practice every day and smooth the week out all the way." That was that. I have been meditating ever since.

Now my practice has changed up over the years. I have experimented with different types of meditation. Each has its own strengths. Each day presents itself differently and I meditate accordingly. I choose the one that allows me the greatest amount of focus. When I say focus, I'm talking about being in the present moment. When you're in the present moment, you're not thinking about what happened yesterday and you're not worried about what's happening tomorrow. You are very much in your moment of what's happening right here, right now. In essence, you are gaining control over your mind and where it is allowed to go.

There are a lot of different types of meditations.

**Mindful-** placing your focus on a certain thing. It can be your breath, focusing on the inhale and exhale. Another is watching your thoughts coming in, thoughts going out, and not engaging them. Counting is a way to focus too. Count up to forty without letting your mind drift off to what it thinks is important in the moment. Or focus on the sounds around you; a fan, birds, nature, water.

**Mantra, Transcendental or Metta-** Metta are Love mantras. Transcendental uses ancient Sanskrit mantras. Inspirational quotes that really resonate make great mantras too. The focus is being placed on the repetition of the mantra, not as a memorized statement but really connecting with the words as they are spoken, *feeling* the words.

**Guided-** Probably one of the more popular meditations. It's also called visualization or imagery meditation. Focus is on the visualization of what somebody is telling you. Walking down a path, sitting beside a waterfall, listening to the water, looking at the flowers, smelling the flowers. You get the picture.

**Chakra-** We have energy points in our body and with the chakra meditation, focus is placed on those energy centers looking to open, clear, and balance them.

**Yoga-** In its traditional form, yoga is meditation, the focus being on breath and movement. Hatha yoga is very mindful of breath and movement.

The idea of meditation can be overwhelming. Where does one start?

- **Commitment is very key**. Start with a manageable plan. I did Monday, Wednesday, Friday. The statistic earlier was that 40 percent of the people say that they meditate once a week. Start with once a week. You can always build out from there if you want to.
  Commitment is key because your mind can be like a three-year-old where it will push your buttons, it'll nag and nag until it gets what it wants. And if you buckle, then it's twice as hard to sit down the next time. If you're going to sit, sit. If you don't *feel* you can commit to meditating right now, put it off for a month.
- **How long will you meditate?** If you are using a recorded meditation, it will be that long. If you want to try mindfulness or mantras, start with ten minutes.
- **Put it on your calendar.** I found it funny how busy I got when I committed to the Monday, Wednesday, and Friday schedule. Anything that is important for you, needs to be on your calendar to hold that space for you. This may have you question your level of commitment to meditation. This is normal. Push through the mind's rebellion and put it on the calendar.
- **Find a quiet place.** One with no distractions. When starting out, everything will be a distraction. Maybe a

room with a door to keep you in and others out. Hang a Do Not Disturb sign if you must.

- **Find a comfortable spot** like a chair or lay down on the floor or bed. I know we see pictures of people in the lotus position doing their meditation or some instructors require certain seated positions. Not for this. The key here is to be comfortable.
- **Decide what type of meditation**. Are you going to listen to music or a guided meditation?

You've committed to the day, time, place, and meditation type. Now it's time to sit.

- **Go to your Do Not Disturb room.**
- **Set a timer if you *feel* you need it.**
- **Close your eyes.**
- **Take three deep breaths.** Taking nice deep breaths, signals to your body to calm down and your mind to focus. Most of us are running around on high energy and we're breathing from the tops of our lungs. We're in fight or flight mode and that is not healthy breathing. Sit and take three deep breaths down into your belly and then exhale fully. You may notice your shoulders drop as you begin to relax.
- **Now the practice starts.** If you are new to meditation, you will notice your mind get very active no matter the type of meditation you chose. Be prepared. **It will be active.** It may begin to judge or say: "Am I doing it right?" "I'm not doing this right." "Why are we doing this?" You start to get a laundry list of things you have to do right now. Cleaning the junk drawer becomes very important. All this is part of the practice. Remind your mind that you are going to sit for ten minutes and notice what keeps coming up.

Meditation is a practice. Each day is going to be different. Some will be quieter than others. Some days you're going to be just wound up because somebody just said something to you. Maybe you woke up from some crazy dream that's got your mind going in a weird direction. Whatever. It's going to be different that day.

Remember, meditation is all about focusing your mind into the present moment, observing where your mind is at. Is it hyped up or is it nice and Peaceful today? Is it happy? Is it sad? How does your body *feel*? If your leg is uncomfortable, stretch it, move it. If you're laying down, sit up. If you're sitting, lay down. Can you *feel* the air on your skin? Do you *feel* your muscles relaxing for the first time in years?

Not engaging, just observing it? Meditation helps us to activate the observer.

But sometimes we just can't seem to quiet our mind down. It is demanding our attention. Maybe there is something in your life that has your attention in a big way emotionally. Do you find yourself lying in bed until 3-4 a.m. because your mind won't turn off? Now it is time for your journaling practice to begin.

## The Art of Journaling

Ahhh, the art of journaling. Journaling and meditation are quite similar, and maybe we will start there.

- **Health benefits**: Cambridge has found journaling fifteen to twenty minutes, three times a week will improve memory, blood pressure, mood, working memory, and your health.[6]
- **Helps to focus the mind and activate the observer.**
- **It is a practice**. Each day is different.
- **Best done alone and in a quiet place.**

- **Different types of journaling**: Free Writing, Dream, Gratitude, Doodling, and Automatic.

Journaling and meditation can be done on their own, but when they are combined, an interesting thing starts to happen. Each accentuates the other and your practice goes deeper into Knowing The Game. Before meditation, journaling can quiet the mind. During meditation, journaling can help to remember inspirational thoughts that may come through and may be hard to remember afterward. At the end of meditation, journaling can embellish the good-*feeling* emotions and thoughts in a more physical way.

My journaling story didn't involve the same struggle to start as meditating did. I really wasn't thinking about journaling at all, much less as a part of my practice. Yet, it turned out to be a very powerful piece of the puzzle. It was 2, maybe 3 a.m., and I kept tossing and turning. My brain just kept going over an incident that had happened that day. It was a deeply hurtful situation and my mind wouldn't let it go. In the midst of turning the scenario over and over, I felt the nudge to sit and write. I wasn't sure where that suggestion came from and I didn't want to get out of bed. Then I heard, "It's not like you're going to be sleeping anytime soon." I couldn't really argue with that rationale. I did want to get some sleep, and soon, because I would need to be at the office early.

Off to the kitchen table I went, sitting with pen and paper, and started writing about the incident. The writing shifted to other topics. It was almost like I was having a conversation with someone. Two hours and many pages later there was nothing left to write. My mind was quiet and I felt very sleepy and ready to get some rest. I slept surprisingly well and felt rested when I woke up.

That morning's meditation, the incident was front and center in my mind again. I felt the urge to write. I got my paper and pen and started writing. The emotions were different this time and the conversation went in other directions. When I felt like it was complete, I sat in silence for my meditation. For the first time ever, my mind was quiet and oddly content. So began my journey of understanding my mind and its role in my life.

In Part Two, I introduced you to the mind, one of the players in this Game. I suggested that it is very much like a three-year-old child. Now, you wouldn't yell at or ignore your child, would you? Yet we do it to our minds every day, especially when we try to meditate. We shut it down in mid-sentence and we have been doing it for so long, we don't even know we are doing it half the time. Journaling is the perfect medium to hear your child. The mind is very preoccupied with survival and can be very fearful based on the diet of thoughts it has been fed up to this point in life. Remember, it only knows the past and can be very fearful of the future. Your mind only wants to be heard. It wants to share with you those fears. Funny thing that happens: once it is heard, it quiets down and you *feel* a content *feeling*. Sometimes we *feel* that to have a spiritual practice, we need to stay positive and don't want to hear the fearful stuff. Listen. You must listen to what your mind has to say and what it has to say in its entirety. Listening to your mind in this way can be a little shocking, to see what it has been holding onto for many years. Mind you, we are not digging up stuff, just listening to what comes up.

There are people who have said to me, "Gwen, if I put it on paper, doesn't that make it so?" usually in reference to the Law of Attraction. No. What makes it so is those thoughts that keep playing in your head over and over and over. You cannot begin to change the energy of what you are attracting without knowing what the thought is first. Once you begin to know what's going on in your mind, you can start to change up those thoughts. And as you change up those thoughts, your point of attraction changes, and you begin to attract the things that you really do want because now you've cleared up the fearful thoughts that have kept those things from you. Whew! That is a big chunk of The Game right there.

What I Love best about journaling is my meditations get really quiet. My days get really quiet. Yours will too. It *feels* strange to not have that whirring of thoughts going all the time.

I hope you are curious as to what types of journaling there are. Below are a handful to begin playing with.

- **Free Writing-** I encourage all of my students to use this. It's simple and straightforward. Free writing is just like it sounds. There's no rules. You're just writing whatever's on your mind. Don't worry about the grammar, spelling, or punctuation. The focus is on listening to what thoughts are in your head in the moment and putting it on the paper.

- **Dream-** As it implies, keep your journal and writing utensil next to the bed so that you can record your dreams as they happen during the night or first thing in the morning.

- **Gratitude-** The focus is on things that you appreciate. Nothing will speed up intentional creation like gratitude. This is usually a natural progression for my students. As they move out of letting go of old thoughts they move into gratitude for the changes in their lives.

- **Doodling-** Focus is on the movement of the pen on paper. It can be landscapes, curlicues, or light and dark shades. Notice the thoughts in your head.

- **Automatic Writing-** Focus is on listening to Spirit and receiving inspirational thoughts. Conscious channeling, if you will. Recommended for students with a strong spiritual practice.

Starting your journaling practice is like starting a meditation practice. We can save some paper and ink by turning back a page or two and reviewing those steps. Again, I highly recommend that journaling becomes a part of your meditation practice. Make it fun too. Colorful paper and pens. A dear friend of mine uses spiral notebooks and decorates them with ribbons and photos. They are filled with lots of inspiration and gratitude. Yes, I am suggesting the old-fashioned type of journaling. No computer or phone. OK, I get it. It is easier, but there is something about putting the pen to paper and making it move on the paper that is mesmerizing, hypnotic, meditative. The action focuses your mind on the place that you're at and it allows you to move into a nice, solid practice. Besides, we are not looking for easy.

We have looked at how these two practices are very similar. However, they accomplish things in a different way. Meditation allows your mind to quiet so that you can start to hear that small, still voice. It gives us an out-of-body experience. Journaling is very physical. You're staying in the moment on paper, making your body move. Just one more reason they are a good fit for each other.

## Final Thoughts

At the start of all this, I mentioned the nudges for this book have been coming for some time. I would make notes here and there and then it came to a screeching halt as I had family matters to tend to. Years passed. I saw an announcement in a group I belong to about a writing group. Some ladies, sitting on zoom with no audio or visual and writing. An accountability group if you will. I could *feel* the nudge to fire up the writing engines. Now I am actively writing this thing and I ponder it. I wonder about where it will go and if Spirit really does know what it is doing. It always does, but that hasn't stopped me from wondering sometimes. Over the decades, I have gotten somewhat comfortable with the bizarre happenings of life that are completely the hand of Spirit in action. I wonder, do most people have the same experiences? Who will read this? What will they think? Will they understand it? I don't understand it at times. It pushes my limits of reasoning. All the questions are flowing again.

This book has been flowing to me from Spirit and I have not been sure where it was going at any particular point. Sometimes the story would backtrack or jump ahead. A lot like our lives. Editing allowed for more information to flow in and be added. I had moments of doubt and sitting down to write was like learning to meditate all over again. This has forced me to organize my work, personal practice, and experiences for you, the reader, to understand and yet demonstrate through the written word what my journey looked like and to encourage you to follow yours.

During a particularly doubting myself moment, I came across a YouTube video which was an excerpt of Matthew McConaughey reading from his new book *Greenlights*.[7] I felt a nudge to check it out. I gave it a quick listen to see if it might be worth the read at some point. My takeaway in stumbling onto this video was how he had written it. It made me laugh. It may best be said that I felt a little more comfortable in the wackiness of my own book and the confirmation that he is most definitely one of my peeps. Again, just like life, it doesn't hurt to have a little confirmation when approaching new things and there have been a lot of them along the way.

I asked the question about whether or not, Spirit, may have left some things out? Yeah, the whole idea of this scenario we find ourselves in could be construed as a game, but does it all fit? There are some things in life that are just down right messed up at times and not at all "game-like." Explain that, if you will, my Spiritual Friends. I would rather not end this book more confused than when I went in, much less the reader.

> Ah, the old multidimensional aspect answer.

Here is what I got in response to my most recent inquiry to 'The Game.' "Each person plays their own game. Games within games, if you will. Billions of games being played on this huge game board. Yet all of this is part of a bigger game."

Trying to take a non-linear concept and make it fit into a linear platform. From where we sit, some things won't fit. Our minds are linear. The questions aren't.

Remember the words from my professor at MSU? Three layers. First layer, each person playing their own game. Each gets to decide what games they want to play with others. We have the ability to move in and out of games. Some games are fun for the avatar, others not so much. Our Soul isn't judging. It sees the bigger game. I have outlined a way to begin to allow yourselves to view your various life dramas as games and learn to come from a deeper place within yourselves so you have the ability to walk away from the table and move to another game and find the Unconditional Love, Peace, and Joy that is your birthright and always available to you.

I listen, I *feel*, I flow with this life experience and yet the questions keep coming. They get bigger and bigger in their constructs. It is quite 'The Game.'

# In Love and Gratitude, Namaste.

In Love and Gratitude, Namaste, are the parting words of the Angels and Guides before they withdraw their vibration from the Heart Opening Activations. I feel complete in what we have shared with you in this book. If I try to add more, it will be ramblings. Yet a part of me knows that we only scratched the surface of what this work holds for you. I hope you take the time to find what resonates with you. Well, I think that is it for now my friends. Blessings.

# Work with Gwen

———

I encourage you to visit my website, InsightsandIlluminations. com, which is designed to be more of a community of Avatars exploring their uniqueness and their depth of being. There are classes for all levels of spirituality. Spirit has guided me in creating oracle cards, gratitude beads, journals and more to add a little fun to the whole process. Explore what calls to you. Let's stay connected there or through my blog, newsletter, or social media.

# Bibliography

1   Rev. Jack Boland, https://w.truthunity.net/people/jack-
    boland. It was a radio talk show with Rev. Boland.

2   Mike Mearls and Jeremy Crawford. Dungeons & Dragons
    *Player's Handbook,* (Renton, WA: Wizards of the Coast, 2014), 4.

3   Matthew Thorpe and Raj Dasgupta, "Benefits of Meditation:
    12 Science-Based Benefits of Meditation," Healthline, October
    2020, https://www.healthline.com/nutrition/12-bene-fits-of-
    meditation. Accessed 21 September 2022

4   David Masci and Conrad Hackett, "Meditation common
    across many U.S. religious groups," Pew Research Center, 2
    January 2018, https://www.pewresearch.org/fact-
    tank/2018/01/02/meditation-is-common-across-many-religious-
    groups-in-the-u-s/. Accessed 21 September 2022.

5   Keely, "Meditation Statistics: How & Why People
    Meditate in 2022," Mellowed, 14 September 2021, https://
    mellowed. com/meditation-statistics/. Accessed 21 September
    2022.

6   Karen A. Baikie and Kay Wilhelm, "Emotional and Physical
    Health Benefits of Expressive Writing: Advances in Psychiatric
    Treatment," Cambridge Core, Cambridge University Press, 2
    Jan. 2018, https://doi.org/10.1192/apt.11.5.338.

7   Matthew McConaughey, Greenlights (Random House
    Audio Publishing Group, 2021).

# About the Author

———

Gwen Peterson wasn't looking to become a spiritual teacher, much less an author. She was looking for a way to feel better. To put joy back into her life. She had the stuff. New home, loving husband, and comfortable lifestyle. It just didn't seem to be enough. There was a nagging feeling. A can't seem to find my happy place feeling. Then like a thunderbolt, her life took a different direction. She found herself having to come to terms with things that didn't fit into her everyday life as she knew it. She found her happy place and so much more. She lives in Naples, Florida soaking up the warmth and beauty it has to offer. Her now ex-husband, Shelby, is her BFF and she loves sharing space with her daughter, Misty, and their cat, Sebastian. She understands that her journey is still expanding and is content to see where her soul and Spirit lead her. Her days are dedicated to supporting others on their spiritual journey no matter where they are on it.

Gwen can be found at InsightsandIlluminations.com.

# Your Notes

\_\_\_\_